Let's Celebrate!

the ultimate party guide for girls

from American Girl

illustrated by Mirelle Ortega

AmericanGirl®

21 22 23 24 25 26 27 QP 10 9 8 7 6 5 4 3 2 1

Editorial Development: Barbara Stretchberry and American Girl editors
Art Direction & Design: Gretchen Becker
Production: Jessica Bernard, Caryl Boyer, Jodi Knueppel, Cynthia Stiles
Illustrations: Mirelle Ortega
Photography: David Roth, Steven Talley

Even though instructions have been tested and results from testing were
incorporated into this book, all recommendations and suggestions are made without
any guarantees on the part of American Girl. Because of differing tools, materials,
ingredients, conditions, and individual skills, the publisher disclaims liability for any
injuries, losses, or other damages that may result from using the information in this
book. Not all craft materials are tested to the same standards as toy products.

Cataloging-in-Publication Data available from the Library of Congress.

americangirl.com/service

Dear Reader,

Everyone loves a good party! Spending time with friends and family, playing games, and eating great food is a fun way to celebrate all the special—and sometimes even the ordinary—days in your life. It's always fun to celebrate birthdays and holidays with a party, but sometimes just getting together with friends is reason enough to do something special.

In this book, you'll find all kinds of party-going and party-throwing tips so that you can have the best time possible at any party, whether you're a guest or the host. You'll learn the answers to tough party questions such as:

- What happens if I get homesick at a slumber party?

- How do I decide whom to invite to my birthday party?

- What if a guest at my party breaks a rule?

Some of the 11 party theme ideas in this book are for holidays, but most are for everyday fun. You can make any of the parties a birthday party by adding your favorite cake and time for opening gifts. And bring your own special touch to any of the parties by adding in a favorite game or creating personalized decorations.

Let's get the party started!

Your friends at American Girl

✋ Safety first!
Some of our projects and activities require an adult's help. When you see this symbol, be sure to ask an adult to work with you.

Contents

SMARTY

Sometimes you are hosting the party. And sometimes you're the guest. Either way, these tips will help you handle any party situation.

Get the Party Started!

Before the party can begin, you must plan, plan, plan!

Getting details figured out in advance will help everything from setup to cleanup go smoothly. Start with the four Ws: when, where, who, and what. First decide **when** and **where** your party will be, and those decisions will help you determine **who** to invite and **what** you'll do at your party.

WHEN: Friday night

WHERE: My house

WHO: Caitlin, Rosie, + Maya

WHAT: Glam-a-Pajama Party

Party Planning Tips

• Certain times of the year, such as school breaks, might be tricky since families may have other plans.

• Talk to your parents about how many guests you can invite before you talk to friends about your plans.

• Make a schedule of what you'd like to do at your party. You don't need to plan every minute, but knowing what comes next will help you have more fun at your party.

• Consider the theme of your party. A theme can help you think of activity, game, food, and decoration ideas. This book has 11 super-fun theme ideas, and any of them can be adapted to include a special celebration such as a birthday or holiday.

MARCH

SUN	MON	TUE	WED	THU	FRI	SAT
			1	2	3	4
5	6	7	8	9	10	11
12	13	14	15	16	17	1
19	20	21	22	23	24	2
26	27	28	29	30	31	

PARTY SCHEDULE

6:00 – Crafts
　　　 – Pillowcase pouche.
　　　 – Headbands
6:30 – Smoothies
6:45 – Dance mash-up
7:15 – Salon + Fancy Feet
7:45 – Eat cake

Invitations

You can make your invitations or buy them. You can hand them out in person or send them by mail. Or with a parent's help, you can create them online and send to your guests by text or e-mail.

Be sure your invitations include:

• The date and time of your party (both start and end times)

• What kind of party you're having

• The location, including the location name and address

• What guests should bring to your party

• A phone number so guests can RSVP, and the date by which you need to hear from the guests

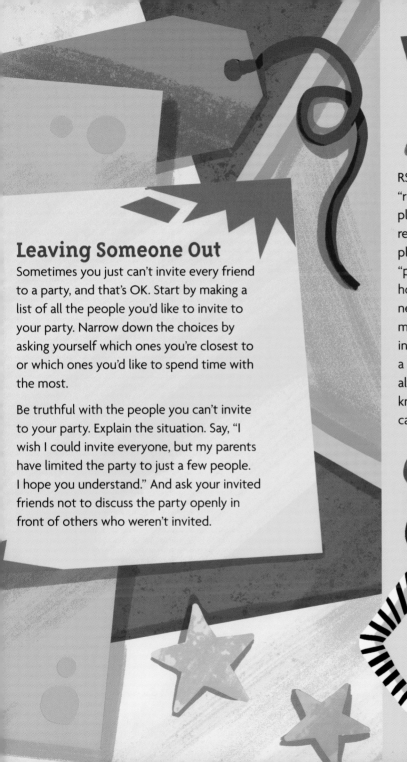

WHAT IS RSVP?

RSVP is French for "répondez s'il vous plaît" (pronounced reypawn-dey seel voo pleh), which means "please reply." If you're hosting the party, you'll need to know how many friends are coming. And if you are a guest, you should always let the host know whether you can come.

Leaving Someone Out

Sometimes you just can't invite every friend to a party, and that's OK. Start by making a list of all the people you'd like to invite to your party. Narrow down the choices by asking yourself which ones you're closest to or which ones you'd like to spend time with the most.

Be truthful with the people you can't invite to your party. Explain the situation. Say, "I wish I could invite everyone, but my parents have limited the party to just a few people. I hope you understand." And ask your invited friends not to discuss the party openly in front of others who weren't invited.

11

Party Prep

There's a lot to do to get a party going.

Make a List

Keep stress in check by having a party plan. Take time to write out everything you need for the party, such as:

- Supplies—cups, plates, silverware, napkins, and decorations

- Things to make—cake, cookies, or invitations

- Things to buy—food, soda, party favors, and supplies for activities and games

Make a Schedule

- Two weeks before the party, make and deliver invitations.

- Two days before the party, pick up supplies and snacks.

- The day before the party, make any food that can be made ahead (such as a cake) and help clean the house.

- The day of the party, decorate, finish food prep, and set everything up.

Ask for Help

Want help hanging streamers or setting out snacks? If you need extra hands to get ready for your party, call on your friends. They will likely be happy to help. Plus, you can do some pre-party bonding.

Your parents will need some help getting ready for the party, too. Be sure to check with them to see what needs to be done. Helping them out is a great—and easy—way to show how much you appreciate their letting you have a party.

Feeling stressed? Preparing for a party is a lot of work. Give yourself a pat on the back for all your effort, take a deep breath, and then relax and have a good time!

Good Times

Of course you want everyone to have a great time at your party. These top tips will make you a party pro!

- Make a point to personally greet everyone as they arrive.

- Make sure *you* have fun! If the other guests see you're having a good time, it will encourage them to loosen up and enjoy themselves.

HELLO I AM...

HAVING A GREAT TIME!

- Make everyone feel welcome. Be sure your guests know how special they are to you and how glad you are that they're attending your gathering.

- Get your guests to interact with one another. Be sure to introduce everyone. If you notice a friend on the sidelines, strike up a conversation and ask some of the other guests to join in.

- When the party's over and it's time to go, walk each guest to the door and thank your friend for coming.

- Include everyone. Don't ignore any of your guests or leave anyone out of an activity. Be sure to spend time with every guest.

Party Pitfalls

Parties don't always go as planned, no matter how well you prepare.

Here's what to do if a guest . . .

gets homesick: Suggest she call or text her parents. Often this will ease her worries and she will be able to stay and enjoy the party. If she can't shake the blues, let her know it's OK if she needs to go home. Try to be understanding—you've probably been homesick yourself at one time or another.

doesn't feel well: Let your parents know right away. They will be able to decide what to do.

doesn't want to do anything you planned: Tell her that you're OK with her sitting out, but you really feel she's going to be missing out on all the fun. If she persists, continue with your party and try to let her bad attitude roll off your back. This is her problem, not yours. There's no need to get into a big argument, which would spoil everyone else's good time and could ruin your party.

What if a guest is breaking your house rules?

Maybe a guest is acting wild or wants to watch a movie that's off-limits. It's a tricky situation, and it can be difficult to know what to do. These tips should help:

- **Don't go along.** Joining in isn't going to make the troublemaking right.

- **Change the focus.** Suggest a different activity: "Who wants to play a game instead?"

- **Speak up.** Let them know you're not comfortable with what's going on.

- If other guests are doing something dangerous, **tell an adult.**

Switching Gears

It's pretty common for a party to get off track. Maybe everyone's talking at once, no one seems to be interested in the activities you have planned, or guests have divided into groups. Sometimes you need to switch gears. Here are some ideas for jump-starting your party.

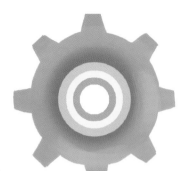

Party Problem:
You're having trouble getting everyone to participate in one of your planned games.

Jump Start:
Suggest a different one. Let guests vote on what they want to play.

Party Problem:
Things have gotten out of control. Mom's favorite vase just got knocked over and people are getting way too loud.

Jump Start:
You need to take control of this party—and fast. Turn off the music and call for everyone's attention. Suggest a different activity, such as eating, playing a game, or doing some other team-oriented activity. If you still can't calm things down, get a parent to help you out.

Party Problem:
You put on a song you think is going to get everyone dancing, but your guests just sit there.

Jump Start:
They might be shy about getting on the dance floor. Get up and dance, and invite your guests to join you. If that doesn't work, switch songs. Ask guests what songs they like to dance to.

Party Problem:
The movie you picked is putting everyone to sleep. That wasn't supposed to happen!

Jump Start:
Stop the movie and do something to get everyone active again—dance, play a game, or get up and stretch.

Party Problem:
Guests are sitting around not talking.

Jump Start:
This is a great time to suggest a game. This will get everyone playing and talking together.

Your Slumber Party

Slumber parties are w-a-a-a-y longer than other parties, and they give a few good friends a chance to spend a long night of fun together. These tips will keep your slumber party from being a snore.

Party Prep

- Slumber parties are best for a smaller group of girls, so only invite your closest friends and friends that you know will get along with one another.

- Create a schedule of activities and get it OK'd by Mom and Dad. But don't forget to be flexible! Gather the supplies you'll need for the ideas you have planned.

- Plan out dinner, snack, and breakfast food options. Remember to keep your guests' dietary restrictions in mind.

- The day of the party, clear the space where everyone is going to sleep. Set up any decorations and put out blankets and pillows so that the space is extra cozy.

Bedtime Blues

For lots of girls, the slumber part of a slumber party can be tough. It's hard to fall asleep when you're missing home. But don't miss out on the fun! Just be prepared. Pack something familiar—your favorite blanket or stuffed animal—to help you feel more at home when you go to bed. Let your friend and her parents know you tend to get homesick, so they will be able to be there for you. If you're really missing home, call or text your parents. Sometimes just a quick hello will have you feeling better.

They're Here!

As soon as your friends arrive, have them set up their sleeping bags in a separate room. Be sure to . . .

• introduce guests to your parents and anyone else who lives with you, including your pets.

• let guests know the rules of the house.

• show guests where the bathroom is.

Night Owls

You're going to be up late—that's a given. But you don't want this to be the last slumber party your parents ever let you have. Be sure to keep the noise level down when the other people in your house go to bed.

Sweet Dreams

If some guests are ready to head to bed and others aren't, watching movies is a good way to keep some people entertained while others can doze off. If the lights are out, remember that not everyone likes to tell scary stories at bedtime. Instead, suggest that each girl tell a joke or funny story.

You're Invited

There's more to being a guest than just showing up!

Do your best to be a great guest. Even if it means playing a game you don't like or doing an activity you've never tried, look on the bright side:

• You're spending time with your friends.

• You're trying different things.

• You're learning how to be patient, respectful, and generous.

It's Not About You

No one can have her way all the time. A party—especially a birthday party—is for the girl hosting it. Guests are there to celebrate her. That means doing what she wants to do (unless it's not safe, of course), even if it's watching her favorite movie for the fifth time!

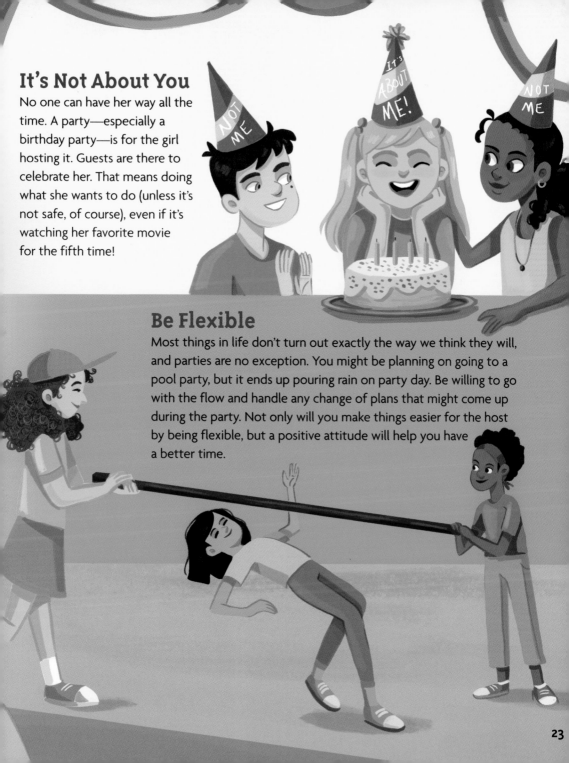

Be Flexible

Most things in life don't turn out exactly the way we think they will, and parties are no exception. You might be planning on going to a pool party, but it ends up pouring rain on party day. Be willing to go with the flow and handle any change of plans that might come up during the party. Not only will you make things easier for the host by being flexible, but a positive attitude will help you have a better time.

House Rules

Every house has rules, and when you're at a friend's house, you have to follow her family's rules. But some rules always apply:

- Don't go through other people's belongings, such as in medicine cabinets, closets, or drawers.

- Ask for permission before you use the TV or computer or get food or beverages from the refrigerator.

- Stay at the party—don't leave without an adult's permission.

- Use appropriate language.

- Be polite and courteous.

- Clean up after yourself.

What to Bring

It depends. And it's OK to ask. Some common questions are about . . .

- gifts: If it's a birthday party, try to ask the host questions that will give you clues about what gift she would like.

- food: Should you bring any snacks or drinks?

- other items: Is there anything you need to bring, such as a sleeping bag? Something for a craft or a game?

Should You Bring Your Phone?

The whole point of a party is to hang out with your friends. So do that—and leave your phone in your pocket or bag. Consider even leaving it at home. If you need to call your parents, there will be a phone you can use.

Happy Hearts Day

Spread the love and friendship at a pal Valentine's Day party!

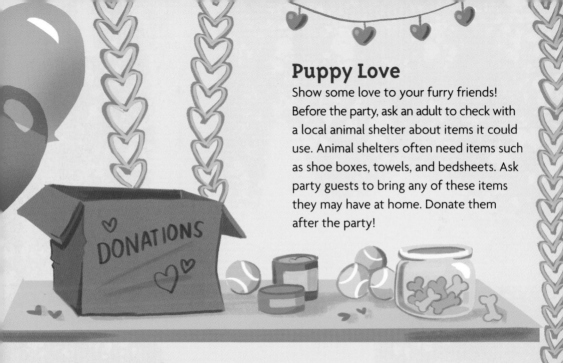

Puppy Love

Show some love to your furry friends! Before the party, ask an adult to check with a local animal shelter about items it could use. Animal shelters often need items such as shoe boxes, towels, and bedsheets. Ask party guests to bring any of these items they may have at home. Donate them after the party!

Sweetheart Style

Start with hearts! Decorate your space with heart balloons and these pretty paper garlands.

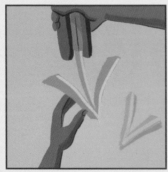

1. Start with a few sheets of colored paper that are 8½ by 11 inches. Cut many paper strips that are 1 inch wide and 8½ inches long. Fold each strip in half.

2. Layer two folded paper strips. Staple them together at the fold. Then staple together the ends of the inner paper strip.

3. Bend the outer paper strip down to form a heart shape. Holding the ends together, add another folded paper strip and staple. Repeat this step until the garland is as long as you'd like.

Cutie-Pie Cookies

Make these treats together, and then share them to brighten someone's day. Ask a parent to help you find people in your community who might appreciate them: neighbors, mail carriers, police officers, or librarians.

YOU WILL NEED

- ☐ 1 cup butter, softened
- ☐ 1 cup sugar
- ☐ 1 egg
- ☐ 1 teaspoon vanilla extract
- ☐ 3 cups flour
- ☐ 1 teaspoon baking soda
- ☐ red food coloring
- ☐ 1 tub vanilla frosting

1. In a mixing bowl, beat together the butter and sugar. Stir in the egg and vanilla extract. In a separate bowl, mix together the flour and baking soda.

2. Add a few drops of food coloring to the butter mixture. Then add the flour mixture, a little bit at a time. Keep mixing until the dough sticks together.

3. Use clean hands to shape the cookie dough into a ball. Wrap the dough in plastic wrap, and refrigerate it for 30 minutes.

4. Use a rolling pin to roll out the dough on a floured cutting board. Use a heart-shaped cookie cutter to cut out cookies. Place the cookies on a baking sheet lined with parchment paper.

5. Ask an adult to bake the cookies in a preheated 350-degree oven for 5–7 minutes. Let cool completely. Once the cookies are cooled, use the frosting to make sandwich cookies.

Strawberries & Cream Punch

Try a sweet and tangy punch! First, gently mix equal parts lemon-lime soda and strawberry lemonade in a large pitcher. (Stirring too much will make the soda lose its fizz.) Pour the punch into glasses, and top each serving with a scoop of vanilla ice cream. Stir until the ice cream starts to melt and turn foamy. Serve with a spoon and a straw.

Winning Words

Play a valentine version of bingo. Give each player a piece of paper and a small clean jar with a lid. Each player should draw a grid of 25 squares on her paper. (You can also use bingo cards for this game.) To begin, each player puts a candy conversation heart (word side up) on each square of her grid. One girl is the caller and has a bowl of candy hearts. The caller picks a candy heart out of the bowl and reads it out loud. For example, she might pick "Be Mine." Any player who has a "Be Mine" heart on her grid should remove it and place it in her jar. The first player to clear a line across, diagonally, or down wins.

Buddy Bracelets

Celebrate friendship with these striped bracelets.

1. Cut 4 pieces of floss that are each 22 inches long. (Use two or more colors.) Gather the floss together and tie a knot at each end, leaving a ½-inch tail at the top and bottom. Secure one end to a clipboard to hold in place.

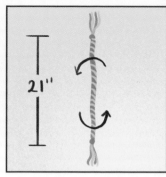

2. Pinch the bottom knot between your fingers and twist the floss. Continue twisting until the strands are tight. Keep holding the bottom knot while you move on to step 3.

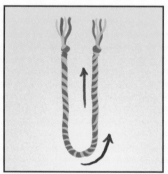

3. Place a finger from your other hand halfway up the twisted floss to mark the middle. Bring the bottom knot up to meet the top knot. Pull the tail out of the clipboard while pinching both knots together. Let go of the middle with your other hand so the floss twists on itself.

4. To smooth out kinks, gently pull on the bottom and smooth the floss with your fingers. The top and bottom knot should now be side by side. Tie a third larger knot directly below them.

Tip: To wear, push a finger through the unknotted end to make a loop. Wrap the bracelet around a wrist and pull the knot through the loop. For a smaller bracelet, make a second knot.

Nice Notes

Spread kindness in your neighborhood. Ask for permission to write and draw encouraging messages on the sidewalk with chalk where other people will see them. Think about the things you might say to a friend, such as: "Have a great day!" or "You can do it!" You can also leave encouraging notes indoors where family and friends will find them. Write the notes on slips of paper, and hide them in books, drawers, or cupboards.

Valentine Favors

Send guests home with a jar of hearts. Decorate the lids of the candy jars from the Winning Words game. Place a festive cupcake liner upside down on top of each jar. Hold the liner in place by tying a ribbon around it. ★

Glam-a-Pajama

It's a slumber party full of sparkle and smiles!

Invitation

Cut pajama pants shapes from patterned paper, and cut T-shirt shapes from plain paper. Glue a T-shirt to a pair of pants, and write the party info on the T-shirt. Ask guests to bring flip-flops and a pillowcase to use for crafts.

YOU'RE INVITED TO A GLAM-A-PAJAMA PARTY! At Asha's house 6 PM See you there!

YOU'RE INVITED TO A GLAM-A-PAJAMA PARTY! At Asha's house 6 PM You there!

YOU'RE INVITED TO A GLAM-A-PAJAMA PARTY! At Asha's house 6 PM See you there!

Colorful Cake

Turn a plain cake into a masterpiece! Press colorful candies and sprinkles onto a frosted cake. Keep the cake in the refrigerator until guests arrive.

Pillowcase Pouch

Start by drawing a star on a piece of fleece and then cut it out. Place the star on top of another color of fleece and trace around it, leaving a border. Cut out the second star. Repeat until you have four different sizes. Place a pillowcase on a covered work surface and put a piece of cardboard inside. Use fabric glue to layer the stars from largest to smallest, and attach them to the pillowcase. Let dry, and remove the cardboard. Use the bag to hold your slumber party gear! Tie it up with a piece of colorful cord or ribbon.

Sleepy-Time Headband

Wear your hair in a special sleepover style. Tightly tie ribbons into tiny bows around a stretchy headband. Trim the ends of the ribbons.

Party Favors

Get the party started by giving each of your friends a small gift bag filled with glam gear such as a small mirror, a mini hairbrush, and sparkly hair accessories.

So Smoothies

 In a blender, combine 3 cups orange juice with 3 cups vanilla frozen yogurt. Ask an adult to blend well. Pour into glasses.

Dance Mash-Up

Work together to develop a dance routine. First, write each of these words on a separate slip of paper: arms, legs, head, feet, hands. (Make sure you have a slip of paper for each guest. Repeating words is OK.) Have each guest draw a slip of paper. Each girl must think of a dance move for her assigned part and teach the move to the other guests. After learning everyone's moves, turn on some music and put all the dance moves together!

Surprise Salon

Take turns being the hairstylist in this silly challenge. First, ask guests to provide their own hair accessories. Then the "stylist" gets 1 minute to do another guest's hair—with her eyes closed! (Be careful not to pull or tangle anyone's hair.) When time's up, check out your surprising style!

Fancy Feet

Turn a pair of flip-flops into sparkly, cozy slippers. Trace each flip-flop onto fleece. Cut out the shapes, and cut a slit where the center strap needs to fit. Glue the fleece to the flip-flop. Let dry. Decorate the straps with rhinestone stickers. ★

Friends & Flowers

Have some floral fun at a colorful garden party!

Toadstool Cupcakes

Decorate cupcakes to look like woodland wonders. Before the party, ask an adult to help you make a batch of vanilla cupcakes. Fill each cup to the top so the cupcake will have a mushroom shape when baked. After baking, let the cupcakes cool completely. Then follow these steps to transform them into toadstools.

1. Empty a 16-ounce tub of ready-made vanilla frosting into a bowl. Stir in a few drops of red food coloring until the frosting is dark pink.

2. Heat the frosting in the microwave for 10–15 seconds until it's slightly runny. Stir until smooth.

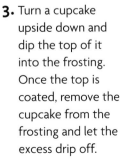

3. Turn a cupcake upside down and dip the top of it into the frosting. Once the top is coated, remove the cupcake from the frosting and let the excess drip off.

4. Set the cupcake right side up on wax paper. Before the frosting sets, place round candy sprinkles on top. Repeat for the rest of the cupcakes.

Tea Time

Set a table for an afternoon tea break. Use plates and straws in a black-and-white color scheme. Then add bright hues with colorful jars and flowers—fabric or paper flowers work great!

Tea Lemonade Cooler

Try a tangy mix of herbal tea, lemonade, and berries.

1. Ask an adult to boil 2 cups of water. Once boiling, have the adult remove the water from the heat and add 5 chamomile tea bags. Leave the tea bags in the water for 5 minutes.

2. Remove the tea bags and let the tea cool. Pour it into a pitcher and stir in 4 cups of pink lemonade.

3. Ask an adult to slice 1 cup of strawberries. Add the strawberries to the pitcher.

4. Place the tea lemonade in the refrigerator until chilled.

Fairy-Tale Flowers

Set the scene with fantastical flowers.
Use these paper blooms as party decorations.

  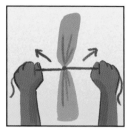 

1. Stack seven sheets of colored tissue paper and lay them flat. Accordion-fold the sheets together.

2. Use scissors to round off each end of the folded paper.

3. Use a 12-inch string to tightly tie a double knot at the center of the folded paper.

4. Gently peel each layer of tissue paper toward the center to make a pom-pom shape. Now you have a beautiful blossom!

Garden Garland

Create an old-fashioned garland with a modern look. Start with a length of string and a stack of paper doilies in bold colors. Starting at one end of the string, fold a doily in half around it. Attach the two halves of the doily together using double-sided tape. Continue attaching doilies a few inches apart along the string. Once the garland is the length you want, ask an adult to help you hang it.

Fresh-Picked Snacks

For a straight-from-the-garden snack, serve fresh veggies. Start with a clean, unused flower pot that doesn't have a hole in the bottom. Put 1 to 2 tablespoons of hummus or dip in the bottom of the pot. Then place carrot sticks, broccoli, and cauliflower inside.

Wall Garden

Start by covering your work surface and placing a pile of fake flowers and leaves in the center of the work space. Give each guest a 3D cardboard letter that's her initial (available at craft stores). Before you begin, ask an adult to use scissors to remove the top of each letter. Paint the sides of the letters with nontoxic acrylic paint. Let dry completely. Then have each guest fill her letter with fake flowers and greenery, gluing them in place with craft glue. Let dry.

Beautiful Blossoms

Use these paper flowers to create summery accessories.

1. For each flower, you'll need 7 small circles of tissue paper. Fold a sheet of tissue paper a few times to make it thick and use a circle-shaped punch.

2. Stack 7 paper circles, and staple them together in the center.

3. Separate each layer of tissue paper by pulling it up and fluffing it a bit.

4. Use craft glue to attach the paper blossoms to headbands and clips. Let dry before wearing.

Flower Crown Toss

Before the party, decorate 10 unopened water bottles with decorative tape. Write a different number on the cap of each bottle. To play the game, set the bottles in rows. Take turns tossing a flower crown headband over the bottles. After three tries each, see who has the most points!

Lawn Bowling

For this game, reuse the water bottles from the Flower Crown Toss, or make a second set. When you're ready to play, set the bottles in a triangle shape on the lawn. Use a rubber ball and take turns trying to knock them down. Keep score as in regular bowling.

Garden To-Go

Create a tiny terrarium! Give each guest a small clean jar. Wrap the base of the jar with decorative tape. Place a layer of stones in the bottom. Next, add a layer of craft moss (available at craft stores). Make mini toadstools or creatures using nontoxic air-dry clay. Note: Craft moss is dried and does not need water or sunlight.

Grow-Home Gifts

Give each guest a berry basket (available at craft stores) to carry her terrarium and flower accessories. Add flower seeds so she can grow a garden of her own! ★

Starstruck Sleepover

**Reach for the stars (and planets)
at a space-themed party!**

Galaxy Garlands

Before the party, decorate your space! For each garland,
you'll need a piece of string that's about 5 feet long. Use cookie
cutters to trace stars and circles on glitter paper. (You can also use a
paper punch.) To assemble the garland, sandwich the string between
two stars or circles, and use double-sided tape to hold in place. Repeat
with the rest of the shapes until you have enough garlands to
create a backdrop. Ask an adult to help you hang the garlands.

Planet Pops

 Make cake pops that look like celestial orbs.

1. A day before the party, make a 9-by-13-inch cake using a cake mix. (The cake needs to dry out.) Once the cake is slightly dry, break it into pieces and place in a large bowl. Using clean hands, crumble the cake into tiny bits.

2. Add ¼ cup ready-made frosting to the bowl and stir in with the crumbs. Use your hands to roll the mixture into 1-inch balls. Press a lollipop stick into each cake ball and place them on a tray covered with wax paper. Place the pops in the freezer for 10 minutes.

3. Meanwhile, make the candy coating. Pour 1 cup colored candy melts in a microwave-safe bowl. Microwave on high, stirring every 30 seconds until melted. Stir until smooth.

4. Dip each cake pop into the melted candy and slowly spin to cover all the cake. Lift out, hold the cake pop upside down, and let the extra candy drip back into the bowl. Place the cake pops in a solid foam block until the candy hardens.

Little Dippers

Serve up some stellar snacks! Bake these munchies right before the party. First, preheat the oven to 400 degrees. Unroll a sheet of thawed puff pastry dough on a floured cutting board. Cut out star and moon shapes using small cookie cutters. Place the shapes on a baking sheet lined with parchment paper. Ask an adult to bake them for 10–15 minutes or until golden brown. Let cool before serving.

Big Dipper

While the Little Dippers cool, make a cheesy dip to serve with them. Preheat the oven to 350 degrees. In a large bowl, stir together ¾ cup cream cheese, 1½ cups shredded cheddar cheese, 1 cup broccoli florets, and ½ cup sour cream. Spread the cheese mixture in a greased 8-by-8-inch pan. Top with ½ cup shredded cheese. Ask an adult to bake the dip for 25 minutes. Let cool slightly. Serve with Little Dippers and veggies.

Moon Rock

Have an out-of-this-world dance party! Before you begin, ask your guests to write space-related words on scraps of paper and put them in a bucket. Turn on some dance music and take turns choosing a word from the bucket. Each person has to make up a dance move based on her word. Keep choosing words from the bucket and making up moves until all the words are gone. Here are some words to get you started: orbit, nebula, quasar, cosmic ray, fireball.

Lucky Stars

Fill a jar with these teeny tiny stars and use it as a room decoration.

1. Start with an 8½-by-½-inch strip of paper. Make a loose knot as shown.

2. Flatten and crease the knot to make a pentagon shape. Insert the short end of the paper strip into the folds.

3. Wrap the long end of the strip around the pentagon, creasing along each edge. When you reach the end, tuck the end of the strip into the pentagon.

4. Use your fingernail to carefully press in the sides of the pentagon. The shape should puff out and form a star.

Nebula Nails

Try a starry style! Get an adult's permission before doing this activity, and be sure to cover your work surface. Use nontoxic nail polish.

1. Paint one coat of dark blue nail polish on your nails. Let dry about 5 minutes.

2. Dip a small, clean makeup sponge in pink nail polish. Dab the pink polish on the blue polish, making sure not to cover the whole nail. Let dry for 15 minutes.

3. Dip a toothpick in white nail polish and make tiny dots on top of the pink and blue layers. Let dry.

Rocket Favors

When it's time to blast off, give your guests these rocket party favors. Assemble them before the party.

1. Cut a piece of scrapbook paper that will completely cover a cardboard tube. Wrap the paper around the tube and tape in place.

2. Cut a 3-inch circle from scrapbook paper. Cut a slit just to the center of the circle. Overlap the paper circle until it forms a cone shape. Tape the cone to hold it together.

3. Use craft glue to attach the cone to the top of the paper tube. Let dry.

4. Wrap treats and favors in a cellophane treat bag and close the end with a twist tie. Place the bag inside the tube so the end of the bag sticks out.

Sea Spree

**Make a splash with an
ocean-themed party!**

Fish, Fish, Shark!

Use a sponge to play a wet version of Duck, Duck, Goose. Drip on the "fish" and drench the "shark"!

Dolphin Challenge

In this game, each guest takes a turn being the "dolphin." Start by having someone throw a balloon in the air. Then the dolphin tucks in her arms and must keep the balloon from touching the ground. She can hit the balloon with her head or her "flippers" (elbows). Each time she hits it with her head, she gets 2 points. Each time she hits it with a flipper, she gets 1 point. Once the balloon touches the ground, the player's turn is over and it's the next player's turn. Whoever gets the most points wins.

Sea Urchin Tag

Make a splashy sea urchin. Cut 3 clean sponges (4¾-by-3-inch size) into ½-inch strips. Stack the cut sponges on top of one another. Tie a piece of string around the middle of the sponges and tie tightly. Fan out the strips so the sponge looks like a sea urchin. Then play tag! Get the "sea urchin" wet and use it to tag other players.

Fancy Fishtails

For seaworthy style, take turns giving each other fishtail braids. Here's how:

1. Divide hair into two sections. The left section should be in your left hand and the right section in your right hand.

2. With your left hand, pick up a small piece of hair from the outside of the left section and cross it over to the inside of the right section.

3. Pick up a small piece of hair from the outside of the right section and cross it over to the inside of the left section.

4. Repeat steps 2 and 3 until you reach the end of the braid. Secure with an elastic band.

Seaside Spread

Cover your food table with a pink tablecloth and drape blue tulle fabric or crepe paper around it for waves. Add colorful stones, sand dollars, and starfish (available at craft stores). Hang sand dollars from ribbon hangers along the edge of the table.

Salty Sea Snack

Make a fun fishy mix by tossing together fish-shaped crackers, cheese sandwich crackers, oyster crackers, and colorful cereal.

Fish Sticks

These sweet snacks only look like fish. Use cookie cutters to create fish and starfish shapes from melon slices. Slide shapes onto plastic skewers and place in the freezer for 1 hour. At the party, arrange the skewers in a solid foam block. Cover the block with a layer of crushed graham crackers.

Sea Foam Floats

Break up 2 lime ice pops and remove the sticks. Place ice pop pieces and 4 cups blue juice drink in a pitcher. Stir the juice until the ice pieces dissolve. Then add ¼ cup vanilla ice cream and stir. Fill glasses halfway with blue-green juice. Add a scoop of vanilla ice cream to each glass. Pour lemon-lime soda over the ice cream until it foams to the top of the glass. Surf's up!

Bubble Banners

Create an underwater world with a background of bubbles!

1. Cut a 5-foot-long piece of string. Lay the string flat on a covered work surface.

2. Use circle-shaped paper punches (2 inches wide or larger) to cut out "bubbles" from shimmery card stock.

3. Place one card-stock circle underneath the string, shimmery side down.

4. Attach a piece of double-sided tape to a second circle. Place the second circle on top of the first, sandwiching the string between them.

5. Repeat steps 2–4 until there are circles all along the string. Make as many bubble banners as you'd like. Ask an adult to help you hang them vertically in a doorway or in front of a window.

Coral Clusters

Create mini coral reefs! Ask an adult to melt a 14-ounce package of pink or red candy melts in the microwave. Mix in 5 cups chow mein noodles until the noodles are coated. Drop by teaspoonfuls into mini muffin liners. Finish with star- and fish-shaped candy sprinkles. Let candy harden before eating.

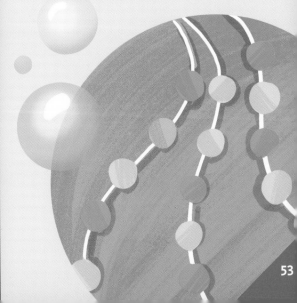

Tide Pool Treasures

Dig for buried treasure at home! Set up this game outdoors before the party begins. Put a layer of sand and seashells in the bottom of a large plastic tub. Mix pearl beads, blue and green beads, and plastic charms in the sand. Ask an adult to help you fill the container with water. To play, each guest takes a turn using an aquarium net to scoop treasures from the sand. When a guest has scooped 20 items, it's the next player's turn. After everyone takes a turn, dry off your discoveries. Now you and your friends can make jewelry using your treasures! Place hair clips, elastic cord, headbands, and craft glue on a covered table. Then try these ideas:

Charm bracelet

String beads on a piece of elastic cord. Add an ocean charm or two. Tie the ends of the cord together in a double knot.

Headband

Use craft glue to attach beads to a headband. Let dry.

Hair clip

Use craft glue to attach beads to a hair clip. Let dry.

Beachcomber

Before your guests arrive, fill small jars (cleaned and dried) halfway with sand. Place a small object such as a seashell or toy sea creature in each jar. Finish filling the jars with sand and tightly screw on the lids. When it's time to play, give each guest a piece of paper, a pencil, and a jar. Ask an adult to be the timer. On "Go!" each player has 20 seconds to figure out what's inside her jar and write her answer on the paper. When time's up, everyone passes her jar to the left and the timer is reset. The game continues until everyone has had a chance to guess each jar's contents. At the end, whoever has the most correct answers wins!

Favors

Give mini dive bags to your guests to take home their ocean treasures. Ask an adult to help you cut colorful netting (available at fabric stores) into 12-inch squares. Place party favors in the center— swim goggles, a sparkly seashell, a small bottle of bubbles. Then gather the corners together and tie a piece of colorful cord around the netting. ★

Hello, Summer!

Kick off summer with an end-of-the-year party!

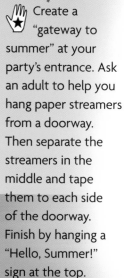

Party Portal

Create a "gateway to summer" at your party's entrance. Ask an adult to help you hang paper streamers from a doorway. Then separate the streamers in the middle and tape them to each side of the doorway. Finish by hanging a "Hello, Summer!" sign at the top.

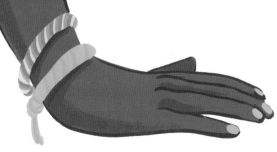

Buddy Bracelets

Make friendship bracelets during the party, and wear them when you're apart over the summer.

 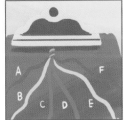 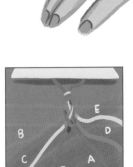 

1. Choose three colors of embroidery floss. Measure and cut six 24-inch pieces, two of each color. Group the pieces together and fold in half. Tie a knot to form a loop.

2. Attach the loop to a clipboard. Separate the strands as shown.

3. Starting with strand A, bring it over strands B and C, and alongside D. Then bring strand F over strands E, D, and A and along-side C, as shown.

4. Repeat the weaving sequence in step 3, always starting with the left outermost strand, followed by the right. Continue until the bracelet is long enough to wrap around your wrist. Tie all the strands in a knot. To fasten, thread the knot through the loop.

Sunshine Sipper

 Mix up tropical lemonade for a refreshing drink. Pour 8 cups lemonade and 1 cup pineapple juice into a pitcher. Then stir in 1½ cups fresh pineapple chunks, ½ cup mango chunks, and a few lime slices. (Ask an adult to help you with any slicing.)

Ice Cream Cupcakes

 Serve a summertime treat with a special surprise—there's a cupcake inside!

1. Preheat oven to 350 degrees. Follow the directions on a box of cake mix to make the batter.

2. For less mess, pour the batter into a food-safe squeeze bottle. Then fill flat-bottomed ice cream cones (just the lower section of cone) and place in a mini muffin tin.

3. Ask an adult to bake the cupcakes for 20–25 minutes. Let the cupcakes cool completely.

4. At the party, put a scoop of ice cream on each cupcake and top with sprinkles. Serve immediately.

Towel Toss

Make a splash! Divide guests into pairs and give each pair a beach towel. Each partner holds one end of the towel. Have a second team with a beach towel stand a few feet away from the first. Toss a water balloon back and forth using the towel. Each time a team catches the balloon without breaking it, the teams should move a little farther apart. The winners are the partners who don't drop or break the water balloon.

Ocean Motion

Turn up the summer sounds! Play musical chairs but use beach towels instead. Start with one fewer towel than the number of players, and lay the towels in a row. Ask an adult to start and stop the music. When the music stops, each person finds a towel to stand on (no sharing). Whoever doesn't claim a towel is out. Keep playing until one person is left.

Scuttle Soccer

Play ocean-style soccer. Divide into two teams and set up a goal at each end of the yard. Play soccer, but with a twist—all players have to crab-walk instead of run! Set a timer, and the team that scores the most goals after the set time wins.

Photo Fun

Take funny photos to share after the party. Create a backdrop with paper streamers or other paper decor. Use summer props (available at party supply stores) like giant sunglasses, snorkel masks, and flower leis!

Sign Off

Send each friend home with a school-year souvenir! Give each guest a solid-colored bandanna. During the party, set up an autograph table and take turns signing each other's bandannas with colorful fabric markers. (Be sure to cover the table to protect the surface.) When the party's over, guests can use the bandannas as room decorations. ★

Game On!

Summer's the perfect time for these outdoor challenges!

Victory Bracelets

Before you begin, give each player a length of leather cord for a bracelet. Have colored beads on hand to represent the challenges you'll do (each challenge gets its own color) and special beads for the winner of each challenge. Each person who participates in a challenge gets a colored bead, and the winner gets the victory bead. Collect the beads on your bracelets as you play.

S'more Bars

 Take a break with a classic summer treat! Make these bars a day ahead.

- 8 cups graham cereal
- 1 cup chocolate chips
- 6 tablespoons butter
- 4½ cups mini marshmallows
- 1 teaspoon vanilla extract

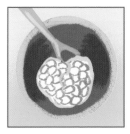

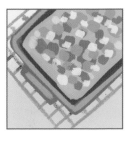

1. Pour cereal and ½ cup of the chocolate chips into a large mixing bowl and set aside. Using the microwave, melt the butter in a small bowl. Stir in 4 cups of the marshmallows and the vanilla extract.

2. Microwave the marshmallow mixture until melted, stirring every 30 seconds. Ask an adult to pour the marshmallow mixture over the cereal and chocolate chips. Stir until all the cereal is coated.

3. Pour the mixture into a greased 9-by-13-inch pan. Sprinkle the remaining marshmallows and chocolate chips on top. Use a buttered spoon to spread the mixture in the pan. Let cool before serving.

Snack Stop

Take time to refuel with make-your-own trail mix. Start with a clean plastic container that's divided into compartments and has a lid. Before heading outside, fill each compartment with bite-sized snacks such as mini pretzels, dried fruit, or tiny crackers. When it's time for a snack break, give each friend a plate and spoon so they can make a custom mix.

Disc Golf

Set your course! Play disc golf using regular plastic discs, and make up the course as you go. First choose a safe target such as a large tree trunk or an empty picnic table. Each girl gets her own disc and takes turns trying to hit the target. Keep track of how many throws it takes to hit the target. (You may want to write down the scores.) Once everyone has hit the first target, choose a new one. Keep playing until you've completed nine targets. Remember, in golf the person with the lowest score wins.

Tee Time

In this challenge, two players compete against each other. Place several golf tees in a line about six inches apart. Set up a second line of tees a foot away from the first. Place a table-tennis ball on each tee. Each player gets a spray bottle and lies on the ground a few feet away from her row of golf tees. On "Go!" each player uses the spray bottle to knock the balls off the tees. The first player to hit all her targets wins and challenges a new player. Keep playing until you have a champion.

Balloon Race

For this challenge, give each player a wooden spoon and a water balloon. Make a starting line and finish line. On "Go!" each player quickly walks to the finish line with a water balloon balanced on her spoon. If someone drops her balloon and it doesn't break, she places it back on the spoon and keeps going. If it breaks, she returns to the starting line to get a new balloon and start over.

Splish-Splash Race

✋⭐ It's a splashy race to the finish! Punch a hole in the bottom of a paper cup. Thread a length of string (a few feet long) through the cup. Repeat with a second cup and string. Ask an adult to help you hang the strings alongside each other. Players race two at a time by using squirt bottles to move the cups from one end of the strings to the other.

Luck of the Draw

Each team gets a deck of playing cards and places it facedown in front of them. On "Go!" the first player from each team turns over a card. If the card is a number, it's the partner's turn to flip a card. If it's a face card, the player has to follow the instructions for her card before her turn is over.

Jack: Do 10 jumping jacks.
Queen: Hold any yoga pose for 10 seconds.
King: Hop on one foot 10 times. Switch and hop on the other foot 10 times.

Keep playing until you use up the entire deck of cards. The team that gets through its deck first wins.

Many parks have rules about collecting natural items, so be sure not to pick live plants or bring items home. Leave them behind for the next person to discover!

Treasure Hunt

Explore the outdoors and see what you can find. Before you begin, divide into pairs and give each team a piece of paper and a pen. Brainstorm a list of nature items that all teams must find. The list could include things such as:

- 2 blades of grass
- 4 wood chips
- 1 heart-shaped rock
- 1 fallen flower petal
- 2 different leaves

- 3 pinecones
- 1 clover
- 1 fuzzy dandelion
- 2 shells
- 3 acorn caps

Set a timer for five minutes. Gather as many of the listed items as you can. When time's up, regroup and share what you found. The team with the most items from the list wins. Try assembling what you've found in a cool collection or arrangement and take photos of your creations. (Bring some construction paper or scrapbook paper for a backdrop.)

Jumbo Ring Toss

For this version of ring toss, use pool toys for the rings and your friends for the pins. Be the thrower while your partner is the pin—and then switch. The "pin" should face away from the thrower and hold her arms above her head. Then the thrower tries to toss an inflatable inner tube or other lightweight ring toy onto the other player's arms.

Water Balloon Catch

Divide into pairs and play catch with a water balloon. But there's a twist: Before you begin, everyone uses sunscreen or soap to make her hands slippery. Start about a foot away from each other and toss the balloon back and forth. If you don't drop it, everyone takes a step back and you throw the balloon back and forth again. The team that goes the longest without dropping its balloon wins.

Balloon Badminton

Make paddles by attaching wooden craft sticks to the backs of paper plates using duct tape. Use a badminton net or a volleyball net. If you don't have a net, make a line on the ground. Divide into two teams. See how many times you can hit a balloon to the other team without letting it touch the ground. If the balloon touches the ground on the other team's side before they can get it, your team earns a point. The first team to 10 points wins! ✦

Design Dreams

Have a fashion-design party! Start with studio time and finish with a fashion show.

Design Studio

First, create a "studio" where you and your friends can dream and draw. Cover a table with a disposable tablecloth and give each designer a spot to sit. Use removable paper tape to attach inspiring pictures and color swatches to the walls. (Be sure to get a parent's permission first.)

Before the party, ask each guest to bring a plain T-shirt that she's allowed to cut and decorate.

Inspiration Station

Set up a table for styling supplies. Here are some things to include:

- A sketchbook and colored pencils for each guest

- Old magazines and catalogs

- Craft supplies such as scissors and glue

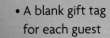

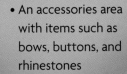

- A blank gift tag for each guest

- An accessories area with items such as bows, buttons, and rhinestones

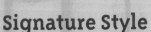

Signature Style

Before you design your fashion line, name it! Here's one way to do it: Pair your last name with a pet's name (such as Riley & Lola, or Stewart & Juno). Have each guest write the name of her fashion line on her blank gift tag. It'll be her VIP pass for the fashion show!

Custom Clothes

Create lookbooks by filling your sketchbooks with original fashion drawings. Try this challenge to start filling the pages!

Before you begin

For this activity, each guest will need a sketchbook. Start with 2 containers. In the first container, place slips of paper that have the name of a clothing item written on each one, such as scarf, dress, overalls. In the second container, place slips of paper that have different types of material written on each one, such as feathers, wool, denim. (You can also include a few silly options such as aluminum foil or flower petals.)

The challenge

Each guest chooses one slip of paper from each container. Then everyone has five minutes to design their chosen item by drawing it or making it with pictures cut from magazines or catalogs. When time's up, mix up the slips and select new challenges. Keep playing until you have a complete fashion line!

Flair to Wear

Bring your style to life! Each guest should start with the T-shirt she brought to the party and a few pieces of adhesive-backed Velcro® brand hook-and-loop fasteners. Then have guests choose a few decorations from the accessories bin. Have guests place one half of each hook-and-loop fastener somewhere on their T-shirts. Then have them place the other half on each of their decorations. Now they can decorate—and redecorate!—the T-shirts by attaching the accessories.

Tailor-a-Tee

Customize your T-shirts by making a few cuts with scissors. (Have extra T-shirts on hand in case someone forgets to bring one or makes a mistake.)

Scoop Neck

Notched Neck

Shorter Sleeves

Cap Sleeves

Shorter Hem

Fringed Hem

Flashy Food
Celebrate style with sweet treats.

Sparkling Sippers
Wet the rims of drinking glasses in a dish of water; then dip the rims in a plate of colored sparkling sugar. Fill each glass with milk.

Bauble Bites
Top mini sugar cookies with frosting and then sprinkle with "pearls" (candy pearls) and "gemstones" (crushed hard candy).

Fashion Show

When the designing's done, it's time to share your style! Create a fashion show runway with a disposable table runner (available at party supply stores), and decorate the room with twinkle lights. Ask a parent or sibling to be the fashion photographer who takes photos as you walk the runway. Wear your T-shirts and share your fashion-line lookbooks!

Stylist Stop

Provide guests with a box of items they can use to add the finishing touches to their outfits. Before everyone takes a turn on the runway, add accessories to your outfits. Belt your T-shirt, layer it over leggings, add a hat, or stack some bracelets on your wrist. ★

Movie Magic

Celebrate under the stars at
an outdoor movie party!

Invitation

Send a shooting star! Use a stencil to draw a large star on a piece of gold glitter card stock. Cut out the star and write the party details on the plain side. Use a hole punch to make five holes along one side of the star. Fold a 10-inch piece of ribbon in half and tie it to one of the holes. Repeat with four more pieces of ribbon and the other four holes.

Movie Marquee

Make a movie marquee using black poster board. Use colored duct tape to create a border around the poster board. Use chalk markers or gel pens to write the movie title, showtime, and any other info you want your guests to know. Place the sign near the party's entrance.

VIP Seats

Set up blankets or chairs so guests have comfy places to sit. (Be sure to place taller seats in the back so everyone can see.) You can also ask guests to bring sleeping bags or blankets to sit on.

Treat Trays

Here's a way for guests to tote their treats. Decorate the sides of cardboard box lids or shallow boxes using glitter tape. Give a tray to each guest to hold her snacks during the movie.

Act It Out

Before the show starts, play a game of movie charades. Have each guest write three movie titles on three separate pieces of paper. Place all the pieces of paper in a bowl. Then take turns choosing a movie title to act out for the group. Keep playing until all the movie titles have been used.

Concessions

Don't forget the food! Set up a concessions table at the back of your movie-watching area. (That way people can get snack and drink refills without interrupting the show.) Serve typical movie treats like popcorn and candy or a meal such as pizza or nachos. Try one (or all!) of the ideas shown here.

Lemonade: Make a sparkly drink by mixing equal parts pink lemonade and sparkling water. Serve over ice in cups with lids and straws.

Nacho Bar: Serve tortilla chips and let your guests choose their toppings. Include toppings such as beans, shredded chicken, guacamole, corn, salsa, and shredded cheese.

Dessert Salsa: Mix 1 tablespoon lemon juice, 1 tablespoon honey, and ½ teaspoon vanilla extract in a bowl. Stir in 2 cups sliced strawberries. Chill for one hour. Serve with cinnamon chips.

Starry Sight

Create a starry sight with lights! Ask an adult to help you set up strings of patio lights or pre-lit LED paper lanterns (available at party supply stores) around the area where you'll be watching the movie.

Screen Time

To show a movie on a large screen, you'll need a projector that works with a laptop or smartphone. Libraries and schools sometimes have this equipment available to rent. Ask an adult to help find the equipment and assist with setup. For a screen, a white vinyl tablecloth with fabric backing works best. Ask an adult to hang the tablecloth on a badminton or volleyball net and hold it in place with clothespins.

Summer Glow

Let guests select glow-in-the-dark accessories. Set out glow sticks, bracelets, and other glow-in-the-dark items near the entrance to your party. Let guests wear the accessories during the party and take them home afterward.

Twinkling Trail

Light a path to the movie-watching area. Set up two parallel lines of clear plastic cups to create the path. Then place a battery-operated LED tea light in each cup. Don't forget to turn them on when the sun goes down!

Let It Glow

Get cozy with your family to light up dark winter days!

Glow Fort

Make a cozy wintertime hangout. Ask an adult to string a clothesline between two points (such as a bedpost and a closet doorknob). Place a sheet or blanket over the clothesline to make a tent. Anchor the sides of the tent with heavy objects such as books. Make the inside of the tent comfy with a blanket, pillows, and LED lights.

Mini Lights

Add some bright spots to your day! Start with LED tea lights. Wrap a strip of decorative tape around each tea light. Use the lights to decorate a nightstand or your Glow Fort.

Shine Sign

Get glowing with letters that make their own light. Be sure to cover your clothing and work surface before you begin.

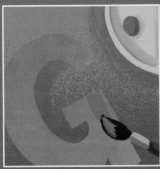

1. Start by painting cardboard letters with nontoxic acrylic paint in a dark color. Let dry.

2. Outline each letter using a paintbrush and glow-in-the-dark paint.

3. Use a foam pouncer (a circle-shaped craft sponge) to make dots inside the letters to look like light bulbs. Let dry. Make sure to "charge" the painted letters during the day by setting them in a place where they'll get light.

Glow Food

Eat a special dinner by candlelight. (You could use your Little Luminarias if candles aren't allowed.) The dinner doesn't have to be fancy; even pizza by candlelight can be special.

Little Luminaria

Let your light shine! Start with a cylindrical vase and some patterned scrapbook paper. Measure and cut the paper so that it completely wraps around the vase. Lay the paper flat on top of a corkboard and use a pushpin to punch holes along any patterns on the scrapbook paper. Wrap the paper around the vase and secure it with clear tape. Place an LED tea light inside the vase.

Day Brighteners

There's more than one way to make a sunny day. Start by brainstorming a list of kind things you can do for others such as giving someone a compliment or helping a sibling with a chore. Write each idea on a strip of paper and put them in a decorated box. Each day, choose an idea and brighten someone else's day!

play a game with your little bro---his choice!

Thank your teacher today.

Stargazing Stroll

Bundle up and watch real stars shine! In the winter, the colder air makes it easier to see constellations. Stargaze together as a family in your yard or somewhere with a good view of the sky. You might want to look for constellations that you can see only in the winter: Orion, Canis Major, and Taurus.

Create-Your-Own Cocoa

 When you come in from the cold, mix up some custom cocoa and hang out in your Glow Fort.

YOU WILL NEED

- Baking cocoa
- Powdered sugar
- Mini chocolate chips
- Add-ins for each flavor you want to make

1. Make the Cocoa Mix

Start by making plain hot cocoa mix for the base. Use a flour sifter over a mixing bowl to combine 1 cup baking cocoa and 1 cup powdered sugar. Stir in ½ cup mini chocolate chips. Into each mug, place 4 tablespoons of mix and ask an adult to add 1 cup of hot milk. Stir until the mix is dissolved.

2. Add Mix-ins

Stir extra ingredients into a batch of hot cocoa mix to make one of these flavors.

Peppermint: Add ¼ cup finely crushed peppermint candies.

Chocolate Malt: Add ¼ cup malt powder.

Sugar & Spice: Add 2 table-spoons cinnamon.

Chocolate Strawberry: Add ½ cup strawberry milk powder.

Butterscotch: Add 1 tablespoon powdered instant butterscotch pudding and 2 tablespoons butterscotch chips.

Starlight Lantern

Catch a falling star—or a few! Decorate a jar to make it look like it's full of stars. First cover your work surface and clothing. Then use a small brush and glow-in-the-dark paint to make little dots all over the outside of the jar. (You can also paint tiny stars.) Let dry. Make sure to "charge" the paint during the day by placing it in the light. At night, it will light up! ★

Sugarplum Party

Celebrate the sweetest season with a treat-themed sleepover!

Invitation

For a tasty invite, write your party details on a gift tag. Then tie the tag to a candy cane with ribbon.

You're invited to a Sugarplum Party

Land of Sweets

Transform your sleepover room into an enchanted land. First, ask an adult to help you hang sparkly tulle from the top of the door for a curtain. (Drape extra pieces of tulle around the room.) Next, have the adult help you hang twinkle lights. Finish with candy decorations: For gumdrop garlands, use a sewing needle to string gumdrops on waxed thread. Or tape individually wrapped candies end to end until you have a long rope. Then tie ribbons in between each one. (Hang garlands up high to keep them away from pets and younger siblings.)

Little Lollies

This sweet-looking craft is a cute favor. Give each guest a 1-inch solid foam ball and a mini wooden craft stick. Start by poking the stick into the ball. Next, have each guest wrap colorful hair elastics around the ball until the whole surface is covered. (Each guest will need about 15 to 20 hair elastics.) When you're finished, tie a ribbon around the craft stick.

Peppermint Steamers

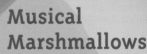

Warm up with a minty treat! Pour 4 cups of milk into a microwave-safe pitcher. Add 1 teaspoon peppermint extract to the milk. Ask an adult to heat the milk in the microwave until it's hot. Meanwhile, dip the rims of four mugs into a little water and then into a shallow bowl of crushed candy canes. When the milk is hot, ask an adult to pour it into the mugs. Sip slowly!

Musical Marshmallows

Play musical chairs—but use pillows instead! (You might want to play music from The Nutcracker or any candy-themed songs.) After each round, make sure you take away one "marshmallow" pillow.

Candy-Stripe Pillow

Make a "delicious" decoration for your room.

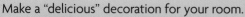

1. Ask a parent if you can cut off the leg sections from a pair of tights. Then cut off the ends of the leg sections so that you have two fabric tubes.

2. Place a roll of paper towels inside one of the legs, centering it inside the fabric tube. Stretch the other leg section around the roll so that you have a double layer of fabric.

3. Use scissors to cut off one leg from a pair of tights in a different color. Cut this fabric into 2-inch-wide bands.

4. Stretch each fabric band over the paper towel roll so that your pillow has stripes. Tie off the pillow's ends with ribbon. Trim extra fabric from both ends.

Swirly Pops

 These goodies look like lollipops, but they're really yummy cookies.

YOU WILL NEED

- ½ cup butter, softened
- ½ cup shortening
- 1 cup sugar
- ¼ cup powdered sugar
- ½ cup milk
- 1 egg
- 1 teaspoon vanilla extract
- 3½ cups flour
- ¼ teaspoon salt
- Food coloring
- Cookie sticks (found at craft stores)

1. Cream together butter, shortening, sugar, and powdered sugar. Then beat in milk, egg, and vanilla extract. Add flour and salt a little at a time.

2. Divide the dough in half and place in two bowls. Add 10 drops of food coloring to the dough in one bowl. Stir until the color is mixed in. Cover both bowls and refrigerate for 1 hour.

3. Roll 1 tablespoonful of each color dough into a 6-inch rope. Place two ropes (one of each color) side by side so that they touch. Carefully twist the ropes together.

4. Holding one end in place, coil the twisted rope into a spiral. Use a spatula to set the spiral on a cookie sheet lined with parchment paper. Poke a cookie stick into the spiral and place on the cookie sheet.

5. Repeat steps 3 and 4 until you have a full pan. Ask an adult to bake the cookies in a 350-degree oven for 15 minutes. Sprinkle warm cookies with candy sprinkles. Let cool.

Fairies in a Flash

How fast can you design a headpiece fit for a sugarplum fairy? Partner up and find out. First, give each pair of players 10 scraps of tulle and a few bobby pins. On "Go!" the first partner has 1 minute to make a hilarious headband or hat for her teammate. When time's up, the second partner gets 1 minute to do the same. Take photos of your creations, and wear the headpieces for the rest of the party.

Bonbon Bracelets

A treat for your wrist! For this craft, you'll need a colorful assortment of individually wrapped hard candy. Tape the candy pieces end to end using clear tape until you have a circle that can slide on your wrist. Tie pieces of curling ribbon between the pieces of candy to finish.

Candy Cans

Send favors and treats home in candy-striped containers. Give each guest a clean cardboard potato-chip can covered with striped scrapbook paper. After guests put their party favors inside and close the lid, wrap each can with a piece of cellophane and tie a ribbon around the top. Sweet! ★

Here are some other American Girl books you might like:

Each sold separately. Find more books online at americangirl.com.

Discover online games, quizzes, activities,
and more at **americangirl.com/play**

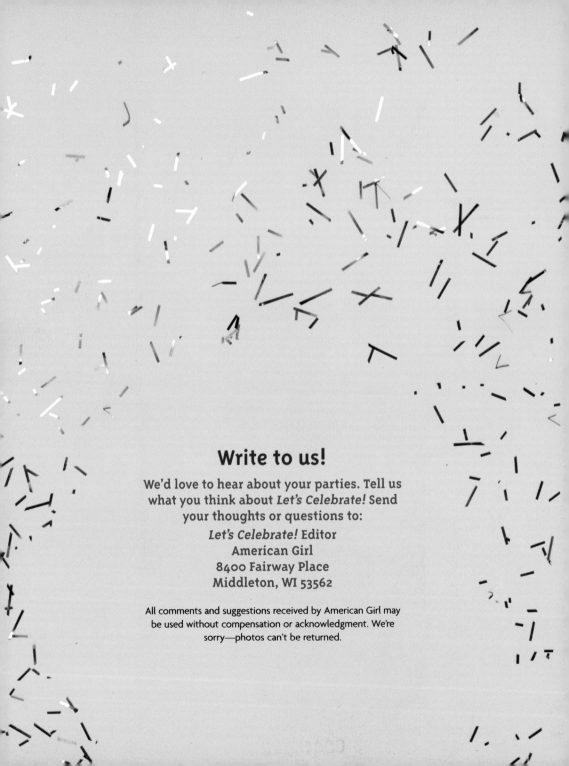

Write to us!

We'd love to hear about your parties. Tell us
what you think about *Let's Celebrate!* Send
your thoughts or questions to:

Let's Celebrate! Editor
American Girl
8400 Fairway Place
Middleton, WI 53562